**1**

**count**

## take a walk back through time, retracing william the conqueror's historic journey to battle

AN
ESSENTIAL GUIDE TO HELP
YOU COMPLETE
THE 1066 COUNTRY WALK

www.1066country.com

**BRIAN SMAILES**

You will never walk alone with these books
published by Challenge Publications


THE SCOTTISH COAST TO COAST WALK
ISBN 0-9526900-8-X

THE COMPLETE ISLE OF WIGHT COASTAL FOOTPATH
ISBN 0-9526900-6-3

THE YORKSHIRE DALES TOP TEN
ISBN 0-9526900-5-5

JOHN O'GROATS TO LANDS END
ISBN 0-9526900-4-7

THE LAKELAND TOP TEN
ISBN 0-9526900-3-9

THE NATIONAL 3 PEAKS WALK
ISBN 0-9526900-7-1

THE YORKSHIRE 3 PEAKS WALK
ISBN 1-903568- - - -

THE NOVICES GUIDE TO THE LYKE WAKE WALK
ISBN 09526900-1-2

ISBN 1-903568-00-5
First Published 2000
CHALLENGE PUBLICATIONS
7, EARLSMERE DRIVE, BARNSLEY. S71 5HH

## ACKNOWLEDGEMENTS

It is with grateful thanks to the following people that this book is published:-

Pam my wife, for her support and help on the preparation and subsequent recording of information and on the walk itself.

Nigel Ramshaw - (Tourism Marketing Officer) of Rother District Council, Bexhill-on-Sea for his help and assistance.

Frank Williams - (Principal Planning Officer) Rother District Council.

*ISBN 1-903568-00-5*

*Published by:- Challenge Publications,
7 Earlsmere Drive, Barnsley, S71 5HH*

*Printed by:- Dearne Valley Printers Ltd. Tel: 01709 872188*

# The Author

# Brian Smailes

Holds the record for the fastest 4 and 5 continuous crossings of the Lyke Wake Walk over the North York Moors. He completed the 210 miles over rough terrain on 5 crossings in June 1995 taking 85 hours and 50 minutes.

Brian lectures on outdoor pursuit courses and between these travels extensively on walking expeditions and projects around Great Britain.

Long distance running and canoeing are other sports he enjoys, completing 24 marathons and canoeing the Caledonian Canal 3 times.

# CONTENTS

**Page**

## PHOTOGRAPHS

## ILLUSTRATIONS

# INTRODUCTION

This walk represents a commemoration and a re-creation of events leading up to the Battle of Hastings at Senlac Hill, Battle. When William, Duke of Normandy landed at Pevensey the countryside would have been vastly different from today. Nearly 1,000 years on, the East Sussex countryside over which he and his army of 7,000 men walked, is still beautiful and worth visiting, only this time for recreation and pleasure.

William and his army marched inland to meet King Harold in what is now the town of Battle. Today the 31mile/49.5km 1066 Country Walk, between Pevensey Castle via Battle Abbey to Rye, offers a unique experience to a modern day visitor as you step back in time and retrace what could be the actual footsteps of William the Conqueror.

Walk now on a journey of imagination and discovery in the beautiful East Sussex countryside. Travel through the ancient towns and villages, over the hillsides and through woodland to arrive in Battle, as William did in 1066, then on to Rye with its cobbled streets and colourful history. Take time to stop in the towns and villages on route, to delve into the history of the area, meet the people and taste the food.

Established links from Hastings and Bexhill-on-Sea are included and these join the main route. As well as the 1066 Hastings and Bexhill links with the main route, The 1066 Country Walk links at each end with the South Downs Way in the west and the Saxon Shore Way in the east, (see links) to give the keen long distance walker access to other established walks covering the entire south of England.

Once you have completed the walk there are buses available from Rye to take you back to Pevensey, Hastings, Bexhill and Battle.

The routes described in this book are detailed and following them should enable you to complete this walk safely. Even though the routes are described I recommend the use of the relevant maps covering this walk to be used in conjunction with this book.

O. S. Explorer 124 Hastings & Bexhill
O. S. Explorer 125 Romney Marsh

Compass bearings have been included where I feel it is necessary but for most of the route careful observation of waymark signs and landmarks are all that is required. Any compass bearings given in this book are given as magnetic bearings. Magnetic north is estimated at 5½° west of grid north for 1998 decreasing by about ½° in four years.

The 1066 walk has both small wooden posts and signposts throughout the entire route. There are red circular waymark discs on them and on the stiles, pointing in the direction of travel as shown below. On the Bexhill and Hastings links there are white waymarkers. Follow the direction of the arrows on the discs. These discs will be referred to as waymarkers in the route description.

Main Route
Waymark Sign

# ACCESS TO 1066 COUNTRY

*SUSSEX*
*1066 COUNTRY*

**By Road:-** The main road serving 1066 Country from the London area is the A21 which is linked to the M25 around London. The coastal road is the A259 which serves Pevensey, Bexhill, Hastings and Rye and links 1066 Country with the ferry ports and Channel Tunnel.

**By Sea:-** The closest ferry port is at Newhaven with sailings to and from the French port of Dieppe. The other ports offering easy access to 1066 Country from mainland Europe are at Folkstone, Dover and Ramsgate. These are served by the ports of Boulogne, Calais, Dunkirk and Ostend.

**By Rail (including Eurostar-Channel Tunnel):-** From Europe travel to London or Ashford from Paris, Brussels or Lille by train. Paris to Ashford is just two hours. Frequent direct trains run from Ashford to Rye, Hastings and Bexhill. 1066 Country is also well served by trains from London's Charing Cross and Victoria stations. The coastway service runs the length of the south coast.

**By Air:-** Gatwick Airport handles direct flights from all parts of the world (including from other parts of Britain). Driving time from Gatwick to 1066 Country is just over an hour in normal traffic conditions. Gatwick Airport is on the Victoria line, offering a direct rail link with Bexhill and Hastings. Lydd Airport also handles incoming charter flights and is only a few miles from Rye in the eastern part of 1066 Country.

**Local Transport:-** There are regular local buses to take you to Pevensey, Rye, Bexhill and Hastings to start your walk. Once you arrive in the area contact the appropriate tourist information centre to obtain details of bus times etc.

The 1066 walk in this book has been planned with easy access by public transport in mind. By using train and bus services you are helping to reduce local congestion problems, car-borne pollution and noise levels in the countryside. Telephone numbers are given in the appendix to enable you to confidently plan your journey and walk.

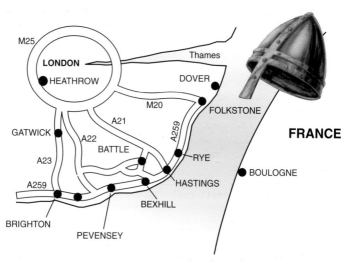

**Access to 1066 Country**

## HISTORY OF THE BATTLE OF HASTINGS

In January 1066 Edward the Confessor died, instead of William, Duke of Normandy being named king, a turn of events resulted in Harold Godwinson being crowned King of England. This angered William, Duke of Normandy and the Norwegian King Hardrada who also lay claim to the throne of England.

It was King Hardrada of Norway and his army who first engaged Harold in battle at Stamford Bridge near York. This took place on September 25th 1066 and in the battle Hardrada and Harold's troublesome brother Tostig were killed and their army put to flight.

On September 28th 1066 William, Duke of Normandy, who was only 39yrs old, and his army in a fleet of around 600 boats, crossed the channel from St. Valery and landed at Pevensey near the old Roman fort of Anderitum. King Harold at this time was still engaged in the north of the country when he received the news of William's landing.

Harold on hearing the news of the Norman invasion marched quickly back to London, then on to Hastings, to confront William and his vast army at Senlac Hill, Battle. Both armies numbered about 7,000 men and the battle took place on October 14th 1066 where Harold and his army met William in a fierce battle lasting all day. This eventually resulted in the now famous death of Harold with an arrow in his eye, and the destruction of his army.

This victory for William changed the course of history and he became known as William the Conqueror. William who died in 1087, was latterly famous for the creation of the Domesday Book in 1086 and for the building of an Abbey on the site of the battle at Senlac Hill in 1070. The battle later became known as the Battle of Hastings because that was the nearest centre of population in those days. Hastings Castle was the first castle to be built by William the Conqueror on English soil.

After the battle, the Bayeux Tapestry was commissioned. It was stitched in Canterbury and completed in 1077. It depicts the battle in words and pictures. The tapestry is on public display, after being restored, in the town of Bayeux, France.

# PLAN OF THE ROUTE

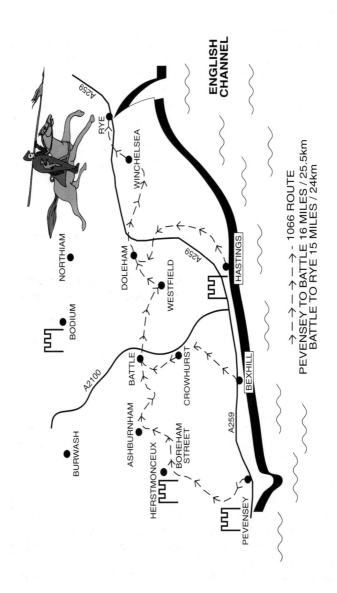

ENGLISH CHANNEL

→ – → – → – → – 1066 ROUTE
PEVENSEY TO BATTLE 16 MILES / 25.5km
BATTLE TO RYE 15 MILES / 24km

A259
RYE
WINCHELSEA
NORTHIAM
DOLEHAM
WESTFIELD
A259
HASTINGS
BODIUM
A2100
BATTLE
CROWHURST
BEXHILL
BURWASH
ASHBURNHAM
HERSTMONCEUX
BOREHAM STREET
A259
PEVENSEY

7

## PLACES OF INTEREST ON ROUTE

### Pevensey

Was a former Saxon borough before William the Conqueror's reign. The village name in 1066 was Pevensel and the main land owner was the Count of Mortain. Today Pevensey is a small village with the remains of a castle (built on the site of the Roman fort Anderitum), 2 public houses, a hotel, and the old mint house, where coins were struck in 1076. There is also the old court house and gaol. The village is situated 1 mile from the sea, as the sea has gradually retreated since 1066. There is a colourful history surrounding the castle and this village, therefore time should be allowed to explore it in detail.

### Herstmonceux Castle

An impressive castle and university building (with splendid gardens open to the public) and one of the oldest brick buildings in England, having been built by Roger Fiennes about 1440. There is a science centre with a collection of telescopes. Nearby is a Norman church and a small collection of houses. The 1066 walk passes close by the castle and science centre.

### Tent Hill

You walk over this on your way to Battle. William was said to have camped here the night prior to the battle in 1066.

### Catsfield

In 1066 it consisted of a small church, mill and manor house. The Saxon name was Cedesfeld. Today it is a small community of houses, a church and a public house. The B2095 runs through the village.

### Battle

Was a small hamlet in ancient times but now made famous by the epic battle that changed the course of history. The Abbey was built around 1077 in memory of the people who died there on the 14th October 1066, including Harold Godwinson the King of England. The building of the gatehouse in Battle started in 1331, but black death in 1348 and

1361 is said to have prevented its completion until late in the 14th century.

Today visitors from around the world visit this picturesque town to explore its history and visit the site of the battle. The town has a wide variety of shops, restaurants, public houses and other amenities and is a popular tourist attraction. There is the church of St. Mary, Battle Abbey and Buckleys Yesterday's World in the town, along with the town model and small museum.

## Westfield

Is quite a large village on the main A28 road. There are 2 public houses and 2 churches, with the Carr-Taylor Vineyard on the outskirts of the village. The 1066 walk passes through the village. Most of Westfield is modern but the Romans once worked iron here.

## Icklesham

Dates back to 722 AD and is named after Icel, a Saxon chief. The compact village has 3 public houses and a church. It lies 2 miles from Winchelsea and within sight of the sea. The 1066 walk skirts around a new housing development, then around the church, as you leave the village on your way to Winchelsea.

## Winchelsea

Set on a hill above the marshes, it is an impressive town of Georgian houses. Planned by Edward I in a grid formation on high ground after a storm destroyed the original village in 1287. With the church of St. Thomas in the centre and the remains of the old hospital, town walls and moat, also a friary, it is well worth a visit. The remains of a sea cliff below Strand Gate is evidence of just how far the sea has retreated. Winchelsea was mentioned as a member of the Cinque Ports by Charter of Henry II in 1155. The museum is situated in the old town hall.

## Rye

Once an island but now a highly picturesque town above Romney Marsh.  It is a member of the Cinque Ports, even though it is 2 miles inland.  Rye,  encompassed by the rivers Rother, Brede and Tillingham, occupies a commanding postion on a hill overlooking a large area.  It has cobbled, medieval streets and that 'olde world' feeling as you browse around the shops and explore the fascinating history surrounding the town, its architecture and 14th century walls.

Rye has a tradition of tile and pottery making.  There is the Mermaid Inn (15th century) and Lamb House, home of Henry James for many years.  St. Mary's Church in the centre, is the focal point and worth visiting.  You need time to stay here and experience all that Rye has to offer.  Other places to visit include the Castle Museum, town model and heritage centre, an excellent starting point to discover the history of the town.

## Hastings

In 1066 was called Hastinges and was a town with the ruins of a castle and church where one of the Deans was Thomas a Becket.  Hastings was a base for William, Duke of Normandy after he landed with his invading army at Pevensey, marching there on 29th September.  Today Hastings is a busy town and seaside resort which includes a large shopping area, variety of tourist attractions, public houses, hotels, B&Bs and restaurants. It has a museum, and the remains of an ancient iron age settlement, on the hillside to the east of the town, in the country park.

There is a cliff railway to take you up to East Hill or you can use the steps nearby. It is worth including the Hastings link as part of your 1066 walk.  Hastings Castle was the first castle to be built by William on English soil.  Today its attraction is the 1066 story which is told in detail.  Other attractions include Underwater World Smugglers Caves and a Shipwreck Heritage Centre.

## Bexhill on Sea

Known as Bexelei in 1066, the town dates back to 772 AD and King Offa. Originally it had a Saxon church and later a 14th century manor house. Bexhill has had many gangs of smugglers during its colourful history, then in 1804 it was a base for 6,000 Hanovarian troops of the Kings German Legion. The town was formerly a Victorian seaside resort and 'THE' place to be. It was the first resort, in 1901 in the country to permit mixed sea bathing. Many Victorian and Edwardian buildings can still be seen today.

Bexhill has much to offer the modern visitor, with the famous De La Warr Pavilion, opened in 1935 and one of the worlds finest examples of modernist architecture. Bexhill is the birthplace of British motor racing with the first race held here on Whit Monday 1902. There is a festival of motoring held here every year. Other attractions in Bexhill include a local history museum, Bexhill Old Town and Manor Gardens, the Museum of Costume and Social History and a Motor Racing Heritage Centre.

A link from the Manor Gardens in Bexhill Old Town to the 1066 Country Walk has been established and a large car park enables you to leave your car there while walking. There is a large shopping area and seafront. The promenade is 2 miles long. Include Bexhill on your list of places to visit or stay and sample all that it has to offer.

## EQUIPMENT AND PREPARATION

Before attempting any walk you should prepare carefully by studying the route in detail so you know what to expect. This enables you to maximise your visit to the area by taking advantage of all that is on offer. Preparation includes having the correct clothing and equipment to complete the walk safely. The route is predominantly low level and you are never far away from habitation and telephones in case of emergency. Having suitable clothing and equipment can prevent accidents and injury and increase comfort levels considerably. If you are wet and cold, or have blisters, you will not enjoy the walk. It is not advisable to walk in trainers, jeans and T-shirt. Jeans can chafe the skin and take a long time to dry when wet as well as draw the body heat. Hypothermia can set in quickly so be aware as parts of the route can be exposed in wet and windy weather.

The following list of equipment is suggested for this walk. It is by no means exhaustive and can of course be amended to your particular requirements e.g. camping, B&B, or the particular time of year you do the walk.

1. Waterproof / windproof jacket
2. Small tent, sleeping bag (suitable for time of year)
3. Cooking stove, matches, fuel
4. Food, pans, cutlery, utensils, water bottle
5. Sunscreen, insect repellent
6. Walking boots, trainers, socks
7. Large rucksack/day sack
8. Gloves, hat, spare clothing
9. Suitable trousers (not jeans)
10. First aid kit, whistle, survival bag, map, compass
11. Torch, spare bulb, batteries

# THE BODY

**RUCKSACK**
*Containing food, drinks, first aid, clothing, map and compass.*

**THE HEAD**
*Should be kept warm, more heat is lost from the head than anywhere else.*

**THE BODY**
*Should be kept warm.
Build clothes up in layers with wind/waterproofs on top.*

**HANDS**
*Should be kept warm with gloves.*

**MAIN BODY CORE**
*Temperature must be maintained.*

**LEGS**
*It is important not to wear jeans*

**ANKLES**
*Should be protected by wearing boots, to help strengthen them.*

**FEET**
*Should be kept well cushioned and dry if possible. Good fitting boots will help prevent blisters*

## THE COUNTRY CODE

The countryside is a place where many people like to escape to and enjoy at various times. To do this we need to look after it when we use it and to preserve it for future generations.

The following is a simple list of do's and don'ts to help everyone enjoy the countryside.

**Do**
- Guard against all risk of fire
- Fasten all gates
- Keep dogs under close control
- Use gates and stiles to cross walls and fences
- Protect wildlife, trees and plants
- Take litter home or dispose of in an appropriate place
- Leave nothing but footprints, take nothing but photographs
- Be conscious at all times of erosion of footpaths

**Don't**
- Play radios etc. or create unnecessary noise
- Take mountain bikes on public footpaths
- Touch machinery, livestock or crops

# ADVICE ON COMPLETING THE WALK

1.  Ensure you have read this book fully before you start and are familiar with map recognition.

2.  Plan your journey beforehand and if possible pre-book your B&B/campsite for night stops.

3.  Ensure you have good walking clothing, boots, and equipment, and boots are properly 'bedded in' beforehand.

4.  Take plenty of walking socks and change regularly. Only wear your boots for walking, changing into something more comfortable for evenings and town visits etc. This helps to spread the pressure around your feet and reduces the likelihood of blisters.

5.  Take a supply of blister treatments and treat promptly.

6.  Ensure you have enough clothing and food for the time planned but do not carry unnecessary items.

7.  Ensure you take plenty of liquid and energy bars for frequent daily consumption.

8.  Be aware of traffic when emerging from public footpaths onto busy roads.

9.  Divide your walk into sections, stopping for refreshments and sightseeing on route.

# 1066 COUNTRY WALK GRADIENT PROFILE

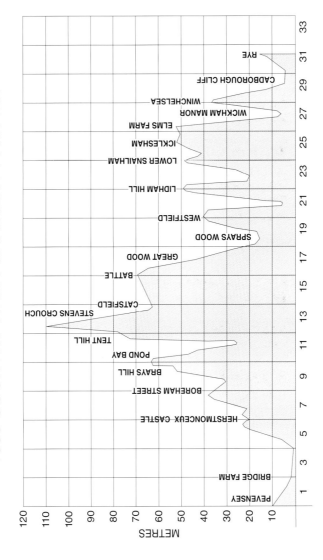

## THE MAIN ROUTE

Your walk starts beside the east gate of Pevensey Castle *(plate 1)* next to the car park. Look for the brown tourist 1066 sign at the castle entrance at G.R. 646048.

Cross the road onto the footpath opposite and turn left following the road round the side of the castle walls for 108yds/100m to a 1066 sign (waymarker) pointing right along the side of The Gables house. Follow the narrow path between the hedges for 325yds/300m. Walk through a five bar gate to cross the A27 road, going through another five bar gate on the opposite side with a waymarker on it. Go through a small gate onto a grass path leading towards a farm ahead. The path winds around the side of a wire and wood fence. This section is known as Martin's Ditch.

Continue through a small metal gate walking along the left side of the field on a wider grass bridleway. Follow the bridleway, bearing 291°M from the signpost and waymarker, **do not** take the path bearing right, across the field to Chilley Farm. Stay by the ditch on your left, then go through another metal gate. Continue by the ditch then as you reach the far end of the field cross to the right side, keeping Pevensey Haven on your right. Look for the narrow but distinctive path across the field.

Pass through 2 five bar gates as the path bends round to the right *(plate 2)*. It is important to follow the course of the river until you are near Bridge Farm G.R. 627069, where the path veers across the field to the farm. Go through 2 metal gates and skirt around the side of the farm, looking for the way-marker at the side of the farm buildings. You emerge onto a minor road at the entrance to Bridge Farm. The waymarker there points right, along the minor road. A short distance ahead is a sign pointing right to Pevensey. Turn right here looking for a waymarker.

Cross the small bridge over the Yotham river, turn left and go through a small gate. The route follows the course of the rivers Yotham and Hurst Haven, on a flat path for 1.9 miles/3.1km to G.R. 633095. You should see a telescope/observatory ahead as you pass through a number of gates. A church is slightly off to your right. Your route takes you past both of these.

Keep on the path beside the river until you see a way-marker pointing right towards the church. Take a bearing of 62°M from the five bar gate near the sign and it should point directly to the church at Church Farm G.R. 643102. Leave the river and follow the path along the field, going left through a five bar gate, along a bridleway, to ascend to the church at Church Farm. Walk through the farm buildings turning right as you approach the chuchyard, following the waymarker onto a concrete path. After a short distance bear left through a wooden gate near the entrance to Church Farm house.

Walk between 2 disused buildings through the grounds of Herstmonceux Castle International Study Centre. Cross a road, and go through a small metal gate which leads into a wood, onto a track, in the direction of the main telescope. Pass through another metal gate, crossing a field where, on your left is Hertmonceux Castle *(plate 3)*. The path is obvious here as you descend the field to ascend again, passing the main tele-scope on your right. While ascending you should see 6 tele-scopes on your left at the science centre. The path takes you along by a strip of woodland to emerge at Wartling Road G.R. 654103 at the side of a car park.

Turn right on Wartling Road, walking to the first house on the left called The Well House, turn left on to the 1066 route again following the waymarker. Cross the stile, walk along the side of the field then along the side of Wartling Wood G.R. 657102 to the far side. You ascend a small hillside passing a large house on your left before descending to the minor road. As you meet the road, stay on the inside of the field as the path bears to your right leading down the field to the bottom corner and out onto the road G.R. 663105.

Turn right on the minor road for 217yds/200m, looking for a waymarker pointing left across the field. Cross the stile and walk diagonally across the field leaving Champneys Farm 217yds/200m to your left. Initially keep by the right side of the field crossing 2 more stiles and looking for another in the centre of a long fence in the higher part of the field. A barn is to the left of it. Ascend again, go over another stile in the centre of the next fence. A sign states 'public footpath'. Cross the next stile with a waymarker on it, then walk diagonally to the lower left corner of the field in the direction of a small wood at G.R. 663110. Look for the waymarker on a stile slightly up from the corner.

Walk ahead on a gradual ascent towards a farm. Near to the barn there is a slightly obscured opening where a stile leads into another field. This takes you down towards the road by some leylandai trees. Turn right on the A271 walking for 650yds/600m to the far end of Boreham Street, then turn left, bearing 22°M from the side of Northfield House which is on your left with a waymarker next to it. Cross the stile, go through a gate next to it then descend a field to a five bar gate. Go through a kissing gate keeping a row of trees to your right. Look for the waymarkers and go through a five bar gate towards Gardners Farm G.R. 671125.

Cross Blackstock Bridge (footbridge) over Nunningham Stream, then head up onto the higher ground into the main field ahead of you. The path bears diagonally across the field heading for Gardners Farm, where it passes just to the left of the buildings. There is a distinctive gravel track leading to the farm. Walk to the left of the white painted bungalow. Continue up the wide concrete and gravel farm track by Tilley Wood at G.R. 669134 before emerging onto a minor road. Turn right here and continue for 1½miles/2.4km on the road over Bray's Hill bearing left at the road junction. From here walk through Brownbread Street, passing the Ash Tree Inn, to just past Reed Wood.

Pass a row of 6 cottages on your left as you continue to ascend. Just past a large building at the top of the hill there are 2 five bar gates and next to them a kissing gate with a waymarker on it. Turn right here into the field on bearing 82°M from the gate, walking along the left side of the field for 314yds/290m to another road. Turn left on the road then immediately right, G.R. 681156 walking along another minor road for 1083yds/1km to Pond Bay. The minor road ascends steeply around a bend where a sign, next to Ashbourne Trout Fishery on your right, states 'Steven's Crouch and 1066 Walk' bearing off to your right between the hedges. Go over a stile emerging beside a house in a small field.

Turn right at the side of a wooden five bar gate, **do not** go through it. The path takes you around the side of a building, between a hedge and wire fence to a stile, leading diagonally across a field. Look for the waymarkers. Continue into the next field and through the five bar gate ahead of you, walking towards a footbridge leading to Tent Hill G.R. 695157. Look for 2 signposts denoting the footpath across the field which gradually descends. Go down some steps between 2 wire fences, cross the footbridge and a narrow field to another stile and footbridge.

Ascend some steps and cross over another stile before ascending steeply over Tent Hill. The path crosses another path but continue upwards to the right of the summit to a waymarker. You now descend the far side of Tent Hill, then go through a small wood walking towards Steven's Crouch. Look for the waymarker ahead as you continue in a straight line to Steven's Crouch. There is a five bar gate with a small wooden gate next to it. Go through, looking for the waymarker then bear right, crossing the A271 road to descend towards Broomham and Catsfield. You pass a track on your left leading to Senlac Park Caravan and Camping site.

Continue along the wide track on a gentle descent through Eight Acre Wood, then Starveswood Bank to Catsfield. You go through the opening at the side of the five bar gate just before Horse Pond, which is on your left, G.R. 720139. Continue on the path ahead to the White Hart public house and main road in Catsfield. Cross a cattle grid, passing the houses on your right, walk along the lane ahead of you to the B2204 road.

Turn left at the road ascending the hill, past the houses, to a row of cottages. Just past these cottages is a five bar gate with a waymarker. Cross the stile at the side of the gate walking diagonally across a field bearing 28°M for 270yds/250m. Look for the worn path in the field. Joining the B2204 again, go over a stile turning left then soon after turn right at G.R. 726144 towards Battle. A sign for Starcroft Farm and a waymarker point down the lane.

Cross a stile after a short distance then walk along the side of a fir tree plantation before following a waymarker through it. Walk between the young trees towards Hoathybank Wood. The path leads through the wood, bearing left then right as you come out of it. Skirt the far side of the wood on a wide track towards Battle. A sign points to Farthings Farm (B&B) where you bear right on another track. **Do not** go up to the farm unless you require B&B.

You arrive at a house further down the lane with a pond and stream nearby. **Do not** cross the stile there but go through the five bar gate ahead, then through another metal gate at the side of Saxon Wood. Ascend a wide grass track as you approach Battle. The Bexhill Link joins the main route here G.R. 743156 *(plate 14)*. The grass track leads onto a good undulating footpath as you walk the last 876yds/800m into Battle. Go through a wooden gate onto a lane leading into the town centre. You pass the entrance to Battle Abbey *(plate 4)* where you should take time to explore the town and all it has to offer. A visit to the Abbey and battleground will be the highlight of your walk.

Walk in front of the Abbey and bear right on the A2100 for 325yds/300m. After passing the parish church turn left onto Marley Lane following the sign towards Sedlescombe 3½ miles/5.6km. Look for the waymarker as you descend Marley Lane crossing the railway line. Stay on the footpath for 596yds/550m after crossing the railway line to where the road starts to bear left, look for a waymarker next to Great Wood Cottage pointing right into Great Wood.

Leave the road through an archway in the trees, the wide track bears due east on a straight line through the wood. As you descend you cross another wide track after 758yds/700m then 650yds/600m further on you pass a clearing where another wide track crosses. Look for a waymarker on your right approx. 100yds/90m ahead to turn off the main track, on bearing 132°M.

You now walk on a narrow path winding up through Great Wood for 379yds/350m to the golf course. When you reach the golf course initially keep right, look for waymarkers which point left onto the main thoroughfare through the centre of the golf course. Cross over the green following the path through, and at a sharp bend to your left, look for a small gate on your right. Cross the golf green again, walk through the small waymarked gate and along the track for 704yds/650m to Norton's Farm.

Continue to the main A21 road at Kent Street. Turn left on the A21, then right after 108yds/100m, crossing the busy road with care. The waymarker is next to a house there. Walk alongside the house and through a kissing gate. Follow a general bearing of 80°M following the path around the side of the field as you head towards Westfield. Follow a worn path in the grass then bear right looking for a waymarker then immediately left in the next field. Keep looking for the waymarkers. You pass under some overhead electricity cables and over a footbridge at G.R. 790160.

Continue on the obvious path passing to the left of Spraysbridge Farm. At a crossroads on the path go straight across on the grass track. Cross another footbridge into a long narrow field, which may be boggy, and continue ahead to the far left hand corner. Cross a stile and keep on the left side of the field. You come to a minor road just past Spraysbridge Farm G.R. 799162. Turn right, walk for 54yds/50m crossing a small bridge, then turn left and go over 2 stiles and a field onto a path along by a tree plantation.

Cross a footbridge, then over a waymarked stile (next to another stile). Walk up to a short wooden boarded path over a boggy area, to climb 6 steps into a small new plantation. Walk through this to go over the next stile. Descend the field to another stile in the bottom right corner *(plate 5)* which is next to a five bar gate. Continue along the narrow path by the stream, crossing 2 stiles, then over a footbridge to ascend a narrow gravel path by the side of a wood. You emerge between 2 wire fences with houses on both sides as you enter the village of Westfield.

Turn right at the top and walk halfway down the narrow lane between the houses. Look for a waymarker, pointing right, which takes you to the centre of Westfield. The path ascends and becomes wider as it meanders through the housing estate. You come to a minor road. Turn left, then right along a short narrow path between the houses to the A28 road.

Cross this road with care, looking for the waymarker opposite, pointing along the side of Westfield surgery, initially on a metalled road . You come to a bungalow, look for a waymarker on a telegraph pole pointing left through the trees towards Downoak Farm. You walk on a narrow path through a short section of wood to emerge onto a sports field. Turn left walking to the five bar gate at the end of the field. Cross a stile at the side of the gate looking diagonally for a stile to the left of a cattle grid. A sign states, 'private Downoak Farm', but you can cross the stile and go through the field keeping Downoak Farm to your right.

Cross a further 2 stiles over the next fields. You approach 2 houses, follow the path to the right of them, into the corner of the field. Go through a gate and along the obvious narrow path. There is a small wood ahead and you keep to the left of it. Cross 2 stiles following a lane at G.R. 825162 in a clockwise direction, to go through Pattleton's Farm. Pass 2 houses on your left, then at a waymarked stile, cross and descend the field. Walk to the far end to another stile near a house and tennis courts. Cross the stile, and follow the waymarker, keeping to the left side of the field on a narrow path.

After descending the field you arrive at the intersection with the Hastings Link of the 1066 walk at Doleham Ditch *(plate 16)*. A signpost points to Hastings, Rye and Battle G.R.833162. Cross the footbridge and ascend for 162yds/150m to the railway line. Cross the railway line and 2 stiles to ascend to a pond in the top left hand corner of the field at G.R. 837162. Follow a waymarker there around the pond onto a minor road. Turn left on the road where a sign points to Icklesham 3$^1$/$_2$ miles/5.6km. Continue on the minor road, passing the road to Doleham Station on the left then ascending over Lidham Hill.

Over the brow of the hill you start descending, when you see a sign for Honeypot Farm and a waymarker, turn left onto a narrow concrete road towards the farm. Keep to the right of the farm walking down the lane. A little further down beside a waymarker at a five bar gate, go through then walk diagonally across the field to a stile in the corner with a platform over a brook at G.R.849171.

Follow the waymarked path towards Lower Snailham. Walk along the side of a dyke/stream just below Lower Snailham then look for a sign to take you up to it. In Lower Snailham go through an opening in the fence beside a house which is on your left. Look for a waymarker pointing straight ahead through another field, along a stony farm track. Stay on this track for 1192yds/1.1km. You pass Snailham House and a B&B near Snailham Farm. Descend slightly to a minor road at G.R.862169. There are 2 cottages on the right. Look for the waymarker pointing to Rye. You turn left along a farm track towards Brook Farm.

Cross 2 cattle grids before Brook Farm then follow a waymarker pointing along the side of the farm *(plate 6)*. Pass over another cattle grid with a stile next to it. Walk to the bottom of the field and cross a stile next to a five bar gate then go along by a wire fence before crossing a small stile into a large field. Keep to the right side of this undulating field. Following the waymarker you pass, walk to a stile in the far corner of the field. Walk around the right side of the small hill now in front of you then ascend the small col, initially keeping right, then going left on reaching the main field at the top of the hill, G.R. 874167 as you enter Icklesham.

Look for a waymarker beside a stile in the far left corner of the field. Walk along a narrow track between the hedges near some newly built houses. You emerge beside some garages on a minor road, which you follow, descending onto Parsonage Lane in Icklesham. You pass 3 white cottages on your left and a public house called The Queens Head, before arriving at the main A259 road. Cross this road with care onto Workhouse Lane where you see a waymarker. Walk on the metalled road passing the village hall on your right.

Just past the village hall look for a waymarker pointing left. Continue in the direction of the church, on a narrow path, passing the orchard, towards Manor Farm. You may see the white tops of the oast houses as you walk on a wide grass path leading towards the farm, which is also a B&B. Passing the farm, look for a small gate at G.R. 882163 on your left with a waymarker on it leading into the orchard. Continue in a straight line through the orchard *(plate 7)*. You should see a windmill ahead *(plate 7)*. Your path takes you to the left of it.

Follow the path carefully through the orchard, looking for the waymarkers, and out onto a minor road which leads to Elms Farm. Turn left walking around a bend in the road, then left over a stile following a path over the hill keeping to the left side of the windmill *(plate 8)*. On the higher ground look ahead bearing 42°M and you will see the end of the walk at Rye (seen as a collection of buildings on high ground in the distance).

*Plate 1*
*Pevensey Castle and the start of the 1066 Country Walk.*

*Plate 2*
*Walking over Hankham Level with Pevensey Haven*
*just off to the right.*

Walk down the meadow, from the windmill, towards the 4 houses on the minor road ahead. Turn left at the road walking for 108yds/100m to a stile next to a five bar gate at a bend in the road, G.R. 890160. Cross the field bearing 80°M following the waymarker, on a worn path leading into the next field, in the same direction. There are impressive views of the coastline to your right. Continue into the next field then descend the hill following the obvious path onto the minor road. Turn right on the road, then left, over a stile into another field as you walk towards Wickham Manor Cottages. The path takes you to the right of the buildings. Walk towards the telegraph pole near the right hand building and cross the stile. Cross a gravel track then go over another stile at the side of a building.

Descend the field in front, walking to the tallest tree at the lower end. You will see the earthworks (town ditch) which were once part of the defences and to your right one of the castle gatehouses. Take a compass bearing of 41°M from the stile at the bottom of the field and walk around the tree in front, ascending the field diagonally to a stile with a waymarker on it. Cross another stile near it then turn left, walking towards the remains of an old hospital (Ancient Monument). Near this building cross the stile to emerge on the road at G.R. 903169.

Follow the footpath around the left hand bend into Winchelsea. Pass the parish church then at a bend in the road beside The New Inn, carry straight ahead. A waymarker is on the corner of the churchyard. Walk to the next junction where a waymarker on the right hand corner points left taking you across the busy A259 road. Cross with care, to walk along a narrow metalled road, crossing a stile towards a 'trig' point, number S6244 *(plate 9)*. Beside the 'trig' point is the remains of a former mill. Cross another stile, just beyond the 'trig' point, and follow the waymarker, descending clockwise to another stile 160yds/150m below, *(plate 10)*. Continue now on lower ground following the distinct path clockwise around the meadow before crossing a small footbridge and stile.

Walk between 2 hedges to emerge beside a sharp 'S' bend in the A259 road on the outskirts of Winchelsea. Turn left here onto Station Road. Look for the waymarkers both on the bend and on your left side. Walk along the minor road to the railway line at Winchelsea Station, continuing over it to a junction, where a waymarker points towards Rye G.R. 898189.

Continue directly towards Rye now, walking along the minor road for 155yds/250m to a house beside a sharp bend in the road. Look for the waymarker on the bend beside a five bar gate which you go through, then continue on the grass path along the undercliff below Cadborough Cliff *(plate11)*. You can see Rye ahead. You pass through a number of five bar gates staying on this path in a direct line towards Rye *(plate 12)*.

Approaching the outskirts of Rye, go through a wooden gate onto a lane with houses above to your left. Walk to the junction with the main road, near a bend, then turn right. A waymarker is on your left, pointing right. Pass Ashenden Avenue and a sign near a bus shelter states '1066 Walk and Gibbet Marsh Car Park' pointing right. Walk into the car park where the 1066 Country Walk officially finishes. To discover the towns interesting history, walk on the footpath to the windmill nearby. Cross the railway line then at the main road, turn left then right at the roundabout and cross the road to the T.I.C.

*Plate 3*
*Herstmonceux Castle with signpost in foreground*
*showing a 1066 waymark disc. G.R. 646101*

*Plate 4*
*The entrance to Battle Abbey.*

*Plate 5*
*Crossing a stile near Westfield.*

*Plate 6*
*Passing Brook Farm just before Icklesham*
*at G.R. 863170*

## BEXHILL LINK

This link was created by Bexhill Ramblers Club in memory of Edith Bitton who was a keen walker in the area.

The walk starts from Manor Gardens car park (no charge) G.R. 747080, nearby is Manor Barn Costume Museum *(plate 13)*. A display board in the car park shows the route and other relevant information. A signpost states '6 miles to Battle'.

Cross the road from the car park and look for the brown tourist 1066 sign at the corner of Hastings Road. Walk along Hastings Road in the direction of the arrow. You come to some railings near Dorset House, beside the dual carriageway, where you turn right then left to cross a footbridge over the main A259 road. Continue walking along Hastings Road at the far side of the dual carriageway. There are hotels and houses on both sides. Look for the waymarker. Just past Southlands Court residential home a waymarker points left along the side of the home. Walk between the houses on a narrow metalled path. Near a small electricity sub station look for a waymarker pointing right, opposite a sign for Portfield Close.

Turn onto a narrow winding path taking you along the back of the houses. You emerge at the main A2036 road. Cross with care looking for a waymark sign opposite. You now continue on another narrow path with fields on one side and houses on the other. A farm ahead is Upper Worsham Farm and your path takes you along the right side of the field towards the farm at G.R.754089. Cross a stile and ascend towards the farm walking diagonally across the field looking for another stile halfway along which you cross.

Head towards a small wood in front of you after crossing the stile and a further stile in the far corner of the field. Cross a farm lane leading to Upper Worsham Farm, turning left by a small house then along the lane. Take a right turn towards Little

Worsham Farm still on a dusty track at G.R. 757094. Pass some farm buildings looking for a waymarker as you descend in front of Little Worsham Farm.

Continue on the obvious track of mud and pebbles to a five bar gate at the bottom of the track. Cross 2 stiles before bearing right across the next field. Follow the worn path as you descend the right side of the field. Cross a stile in the bottom right corner then continue along the left side of the next field alongside a ditch, and crossing an old railway embankment. A waymarker points across a footbridge. Cross another footbridge soon after and walk along by the ditch following the waymarkers towards Crowhurst. **Do not** turn off the main path.

You walk along by a ditch or dyke on your right side. A sign on a five bar gate states 'private', so continue in the direction you are walking. Cross a stile where up on your left is Hillcroft Farm and to your right, Croucher's Farm. Walk under some overhead electricity cables where a waymarker, beside a wire fence on your left, points ahead as you approach the village of Crowhurst at G.R. 760116. You emerge on a road with some stables on your left and a public house called The Plough nearby.

Turn right and continue along the road to Sampson's Lane on your left where there is a waymark sign nearby. Walk along Sampson's Lane then turn left 87yds/80m further on going over a stile beside a five bar gate. A sign there states 'Southern Water Services'. The path winds around the lower side of the field towards Pond Bay at G.R. 758122. A church is off to your left. Look for a small footbridge and stile which you cross, then walk around the edge of the field in the direction of the church, which you should now see ahead at Crowhurst.

When passing the pond at Pond Bay you come to a minor road where you turn right and ascend the hillside for 162yds/150m passing the ruins of the manor house just off to your left. Keep on the road and at the fork bear left

*Plate 7*
*Walking through the Orchard near Manor Farm leading to*
*the Windmill, East of Icklesham.*

*Plate 8*
*The Windmill near Elms Farm on route to*
*Winchelsea. G.R. 886161*

*Plate 9*
*The Triangulation Pillar on the outskirts of Winchelsea,*
*at G.R. 901175*

*Plate 10*
*Descending the hillside around the National Trust Land*
*on leaving Winchelsea. G.R. 900176*

on the road around the church. Near the telephone box look for the waymarker at a stile to cross the fields and take you through the south west side of Fore Wood Nature Reserve on the waymarked path bearing 258°M from the stile.

You come to a new stone bridge over Powdermill Stream as you leave the wood at G.R. 747133 then walk on a path between the fields into Stumblet's Wood bearing 265°M from the bridge. Turn right as you enter Stumblet's Wood and ascend on a track towards Peppering Eye Farm. On leaving Stumblet's Wood, turn right following a waymarker along a narrow metalled road, crossing a bridge then passing the farm buildings.

Stay on this road, passing Stone Cottage, until you reach the minor road known as Telham Lane where a waymarker points left at G.R. 745144.

Turn left walking for 162yds/150m to the B2095 at Powdermill Lane, where a waymarker points right over a stile to ascend the field parallel with the road on your right. At the top corner of this field the path bears slightly left across another field heading towards the right hand corner of a wood which you will see in front of you.

Cross a stile onto a lane at G.R. 744147 which leads to Powdermill Lake, then across another stile opposite taking you through a farm storage area. Descend a rough track to the right hand corner of the wood ahead where there is a gate and stile. After crossing, continue up the well made track. Initially it is flat before rising steeply just before the corner of the wood ahead at G.R. 743153.

Continue over the brow of the hill skirting the left side of the wood, where you meet the main 1066 route from Pevensey to Battle at G.R. 743155 *(plate14)*. A signpost points in each direction. You now follow the main route directions into Battle.

## HASTINGS LINK

Start at the bend in the A259 road near the T.I.C. G.R.825095 at the seafront in Hastings *(plate15).* The castle is 487yds/450m further on. Walk east towards the cliff railway ascending Tamarisk Steps at the side of the Dolphin Inn. Halfway up take a right turn to a row of houses called Tackleway, cross the road and continue to ascend steeply to the top of the hill.

Nearing the top beside the cliff railway, a sign states 'Welcome to Hastings Country Park, East Hill', and just past the sign a waymarker points to the 1066 walk ahead. Follow this onto the open grassed area of East Hill. Pass between the pitch and putt, to the left of the iron age settlement, looking for waymarkers as you proceed.

Look for a brick pavilion ahead and pass to the right of it walking for 108yds/100m to a large sign, pointing left, with a waymarker nearby. Descend the track passing a house on your left to arrive at Barley Lane G.R. 837104. Turn right at Barley Lane on a gradual ascent for approx. 1mile/1700m, passing ShearBarn Camping Park reception on the right. You may see a T.V./radio mast ahead. Your route passes near it but continue up the lane until you come to a T-junction.

A waymarker is on the right corner pointing left towards the mast. Walk along this lane to emerge on a road near the mast. A house is on the left. Cross the road taking care on the sharp bend and looking for the kissing gate. A Hastings Country Park sign is nearby. Go through then bear left along the side of a wire fence between 2 fields. This is the highest point, with good views inland. Go through another kissing gate, there are 2 paths ahead with the 1066 walk to the right. Cross the stile, descending a narrow grass path for 542yds/500m between gorse bushes, with commanding views over the whole area.

*Plate 11*
*Walking below Cadborough Cliff just before Rye.*

*Plate 12*
*The final approach to Rye.*

*Plate 13*
*The start of the Bexhill Link of the 1066 Country Walk.*

*Plate 14*
*The signpost where the Bexhill Link (foreground) joins*
*the main route just before Battle AT. G.R. 743155.*

You cross a stile on each side of a minor road near an entrance to Fairlight Hall, then walk alongside a wood in the direction of Humphrey's Farm. On your right is a stile with a waymarker on it. Look carefully as the sign is pointing left across a field in the direction of the white houses you can see. Looking across the field you should see another waymarker at the far side. Cross the field then bear right still descending before bearing left to ascend through the small wood you can see ahead.

Walk over a footbridge on leaving the wood then over a small stile into a field. Follow the worn waymarked path. Cross a track and go over 3 stiles on a narrow path then bear left to ascend to a small pond encircled by trees. Walk around the right side of the pond nearing the houses then bear right following the hedge down to another waymarked stile leading to Pett Road at G.R. 857133 at Friar's Hill.

Turn right for 184yds/170m to just past the last house on the left called Well House where you turn left onto Chapel Lane. Turn immediately right following a waymarker along the right side of Glebe Wood G.R. 858135. Continue to a minor road called Church Lane, cross it following the waymarker. Now you are on a driveway which you walk along. Look for a waymarker on the right. Go through a kissing gate into a field at G.R. 861137. Keep to the left side looking for a metal gate halfway along with a waymarker on it.

Pass 2 garages as you walk towards Guestling Wood ahead. On entering the wood walk straight ahead looking for the waymarker, as the path gradually bears around to the left to take you out of the wood and up to Church Farm. You leave the wood beside a small sewerage works where you ascend the field and go around the side of a small wood ahead, to Church Farm.

Pass through a kissing gate into the churchyard walking along the side of the church and through the entrance at the far side. Cross the road then go through an opening in the hedge onto a narrow path running parallel with the lane. Continue straight on to the A259 road, where you cross onto a footpath. Turn right and walk for 325yds/300m to an opening into Fraysland Wood. Look for a waymarker. Follow the wide track through to a kissing gate at the far side G.R.849147, then along the right side of a field on a grass path.

Continue along the side of the fields crossing 2 more stiles, to the corner of Plashet Wood. Bear left here 278°M to cross the field diagonally onto a minor road at Three Oaks. Follow the waymarker left for 119yds/110m to Sunny Croft which is a lane off to your right. Walk between the small collection of bungalows to a five bar gate at the far end with a small gate next to it. Go through then continue straight ahead for 162yds/150m to another path before bearing slightly right 360°M over a stile at G.R.840149 then crossing 3 fields. This section needs extra care as it is a little harder to navigate over. Go over a stile then cross a railway line. Just before it you should see a waymarker.

Continue on the narrow path around the right side of a small wood G.R. 835152 before crossing a stile. Descend the stony track where you see a signpost pointing right on leaving the wood to take you over a stile into a field by Sailor's Stream. The grass track winds around the left side of the field then over a stile next to a five bar gate. Continue on the path between the wire fences.

A waymarker is beside a footbridge where you turn right along the side of a field leading to Doleham Ditch. You come to a footbridge where the path from Hastings joins the main route at the signpost in the field *(plate 16)*. Turn right towards Rye or left towards Battle to continue your journey.

*Plate 15*
*The Seafront near the tourist information centre, Hastings*
*where the Hastings Link of the 1066 Country Walk starts.*

*Plate 16*
*The signpost beside Doleham Ditch (centre left) where the*
*Hastings Link joins the main route just before Doleham Station at*
*G.R. 833162*

## SAXON SHORE WAY LINK (EAST)

It is possible to link the 1066 Country Walk with the Saxon Shore Way. From Gibbet Marsh car park bear left on a path towards the windmill ahead of you. Cross the railway line, then when you meet the main road turn left, then right at the mini roundabout. Cross the road to the T.I.C. and walk along the street called The Deals then ascend steeply up Mermaid Street. Turn right onto West Street, keeping in front of the church and passing Lion Street, then go around the church itself onto East Street.

Walk down East Street turning right at the junction with High Street and go along onto Hilders Cliff. Descend through the old castle gates, built in 1329. There are exellent views from this area. Walk onto Landgate, past the Queens Head and Bedford Arms. Turn right onto Fishmarket Road (also known as Bedford Place). You come to a mini roundabout near a car sales room. Turn left to meet with The Saxon Shore Way, which crosses the bridge over the River Rother.

## SOUTH DOWNS WAY LINK (WEST)

It is also possible to link the 1066 Country Walk with the South Downs Way. Walking from Pevensey Castle (east gate), follow the castle walls around the outside on the B2191 road. After 271yds/250m turn right in the direction of Castle Farm, keeping to the left side of 2 fields before crossing the next field following the waymarker to a footbridge. Take a bearing of 268°M from the footbridge to Castle Farm. Walk between the farm buildings heading in the same direction to join the minor road 162yds/150m further on.

Turn right at the road, walking for 1.4miles/2.2km to join the B2247. A church is on your right. You continue on this road following signs for the Weald Way (south). Soon you will join up with the South Downs Way to Eastbourne or to Alfriston.

## APPENDIX

## GRID REFERENCES
### Main Route
| | |
|---|---|
| Pevensey Castle (start) | G.R. 646048 |
| Bridge Farm | G.R. 627069 |
| Church Farm | G.R. 643102 |
| Boreham Street | G.R. 665113 |
| Brownbread Street | G.R. 676149 |
| Steven's Crouch | G.R. 711154 |
| Catsfield | G.R. 723137 |
| Bexhill Link/Main Route | G.R. 743155 |
| Battle Abbey | G.R. 748158 |
| Kent Street | G.R. 787159 |
| Hastings Link/Main Route | G.R. 833162 |
| Icklesham | G.R. 879165 |
| Wickham Manor | G.R. 898164 |
| Winchelsea Station | G.R. 900184 |
| Rye (finish) | G.R. 916203 |

### Bexhill Link
| | |
|---|---|
| Bexhill (start) | G.R. 747080 |
| Upper Worsham Farm Entrance | G.R. 756092 |
| Pond Bay | G.R. 758122 |
| Stumblet's Wood | G.R. 746133 |
| Bexhill Link/Main Route | G.R. 743155 |

### Hastings Link
| | |
|---|---|
| Hastings (start) | G.R. 825095 |
| Mast on Hill | G.R. 847117 |
| Glebe Wood | G.R. 858135 |
| Pound Farm | G.R. 852144 |
| Hastings Link/Main Route | G.R. 833162 |

This section has been included to assist walkers, particularly those who have a G.P.S. system, to locate precise positions on route. You may also find it helpful to use in conjunction with the relevant O.S. map of the area.

## CAMPSITES ON ROUTE

**Pevensey Bay**
G.R. 649027 - Bay View Caravan & Camping Park, Old Martello Road. BN24 6DX
Tel. 01323 768688

**Catsfield**
G.R. 719151 - Senlac Park Caravan & Camping Site, Main Road, Catsfield, Battle TN33 9DU
Tel. 01424 773969

**Sedlescombe**
G.R. 783170 - Crazy Lane Tourist Park, Whydown Farm, Sedlescombe, Battle TN33 0QT
Tel. 01424 870147  www.crazylane.co.uk

**Pett**
G.R. 886143 - David Lovejoy, Carters Farm, Elm Lane, Pett, Hastings TN35 4JD
Booking Tel. 01424 813206 or 812244

**Crowhurst (Bexhill Link)**
G.R. 763130 - Brakes Coppice Park, Forewood Lane, Crowhurst, Nr. Battle TN33 9AB
Tel. 01424 830322 Fax 01424 830758
Email - brakecoppicepark@netlineuk.net
www.brakescoppicepark.co.uk

**Hastings (Hastings Link)**
G.R. 842109 - ShearBarn Holiday Park, Barley Lane, Hastings TN35 5DX
Bookings Tel. 01424 423583  Fax 01424 718740

These campsites are in route order.  There are no campsites available in or around Rye so extra B&Bs have been included in Rye (see B&Bs on route).

## B&Bs ON ROUTE

All B&Bs shown have been selected as being the nearest to the 1066 route. They are not shown in any order of preference.

### Pevensey
*Priory Court Hotel & Restaurant,* Castle Road, Pevensey BN24 5LG   Tel. 01323 763150
Fax 01323 769030

*Banks Lodge,* High Street, Pevensey Village. BN24 5LE
Tel. 01323 763741

*Mrs. Bennet,* Runnymede, Wallsend, Pevensey
Tel. 01323 469408

### Catsfield
*Farthings Farm,* Catsfield, Battle TN33 9BA
Tel. 01424 773107   Booking by prior arrangement only

### Battle
*Clematis Cottage,* The Green, 3, High Street, Battle TN33 0AE
Tel. 01424 774261 or 01424 772416 (Eves.)

*White Ladies,* Starrs Green Lane, Battle TN 33 0TD
Tel. 01424 774261 or 01424 772416 (Eves.)

Telephone in advance if possible for both of the above

### Icklesham
*Stuart & Noi Plumbly,* The Old Farmhouse, Icklesham TN36 4AT  Tel. 01424 814711  Fax 01424 814007
http://members.aol.com/oldfrmhse

*Manor Farm Oast,* Workhouse Lane, TN36 4AJ
Tel/Fax: 01424 813787
manor.farm.oast@lineone.net

### Rye
*The Windmill Guesthouse,* off Ferry Road, Rye TN31 7DW  Tel. 01797 224027  Fax 01797 227212

*The Pink House,* 35 Udimore Road, Rye TN31 7EA
Tel. 01797 227453

*Magnolia House,* 15 Udimore Road, Rye TN31 7DS
Tel. 01797 222561  Fax 01797 227525
www.magnoliaguesthouse.co.uk

*Aviemore Guesthouse,* 28 Fishmarket Road, Rye
Tel/Fax 01797 223052
aviemore@lineone.net

*Shirley Care,* Woodpeckers, West Undercliff, Rye TN31 7DX
Tel. 01797 223013/223999

*Western House,* Winchelsea Road, Rye TN31 7EL
Tel. 01797 223419

## YOUTH HOSTELS

Eastbourne  -  01323 721081
Hastings      -  01424 812373

## TELEPHONES ON ROUTE

### Main Route
| | |
|---|---|
| Pevensey | G.R. 653046 |
| Boreham Street | G.R. 665113 |
| Steven's Crouch | G.R. 712154 |
| Catsfield | G.R. 723137 |
| Battle Town Centre | |
| Westfield | G.R. 813156 |
| Icklesham | G.R. 874163 |
| Winchelsea Centre | |
| Rye Town Centre | |

### Bexhill Link
| | |
|---|---|
| Bexhill Centre | |
| Crowhurst | G.R. 759118 |
| | G.R. 756125 |

### Hastings Link
| | |
|---|---|
| Hastings Centre | |
| Friars Hill | G.R. 863136 |
| Three Oaks | G.R. 839146 |

## APPROXIMATE WALKING TIMES
## BETWEEN PROMINENT LANDMARKS

| Main Route | | Hrs. | Mins |
|---|---|---|---|
| Pevensey Castle to Bridge Farm | | | 45 |
| Bridge Farm | to Boreham Street | 2 | 00 |
| Boreham Street | to Brownbread Street | 1 | 15 |
| Brownbread St. | to Catsfield | 1 | 45 |
| Catsfield | to Battle | 1 | 10 |
| Battle | to Kent Street | 1 | 10 |
| Kent Street | to Westfield | | 50 |
| Westfield | to Icklesham | 2 | 00 |
| Icklesham | to Winchelsea | 1 | 00 |
| Winchelsea | to Rye | 1 | 20 |
| | | **13** | **05** |

| Bexhill Link | | | Hrs. | Mins |
|---|---|---|---|---|
| Bexhill | to | Crowhurst Church | 1 | 25 |
| Crowhurst Ch. | to | Battle | 1 | 30 |
| | | | **2** | **55** |

| Hastings Link | | | Hrs. | Mins |
|---|---|---|---|---|
| Hastings | to | Glebe Wood | 2 | 00 |
| Glebe Wood | to | Main Route Intersection | 1 | 30 |
| | | | **3** | **30** |

**Note:** It will take approximately 13 hours walking time to complete the main route. However this will vary depending on the fitness of each person in the group and the conditions encountered, along with the weight of the pack you are carrying. It is suggested that you spread your journey over a number of days to give you time to enjoy all that 1066 Country and this walk has to offer, stopping at a B&B or campsite on route overnight and visiting some of the attractions on your journey.

# DISTANCES BETWEEN
# PROMINENT LANDMARKS

## Main Route

| | | | Miles | Km |
|---|---|---|---|---|
| Pevensey Castle | to | Bridge Farm | 1.93 | 3.1 |
| Bridge Farm | to | Church Farm | 2.86 | 4.6 |
| Church Farm | to | Boreham Street | 2.05 | 3.3 |
| Boreham Street | to | Brownbread Street | 2.61 | 4.2 |
| Brownbread St. | to | Steven's Crouch | 2.86 | 4.6 |
| Steven's Crouch | to | Catsfield | 1.49 | 2.4 |
| Catsfield | to | Battle | 2.11 | 3.4 |
| Battle | to | Kent Street | 2.73 | 4.4 |
| Kent Street | to | Westfield | 1.99 | 3.2 |
| Westfield | to | Doleham Ditch | 1.37 | 2.2 |
| Doleham Ditch | to | Lower Snailham | 1.43 | 2.3 |
| Lower Snailham | to | Icklesham | 1.74 | 2.8 |
| Icklesham | to | Winchelsea Centre | 2.36 | 3.8 |
| Winchelsea | to | Rye (Gibbet Marsh Car Park) | 3.36 | 5.4 |
| | | | **30.9** | **49.7** |

## Bexhill Link

| | | | Miles | Km |
|---|---|---|---|---|
| Bexhill Car park | to | Crowhurst Church | 3.3 | 5.3 |
| Crowhurst Church | to | Battle | 2.92 | 4.7 |
| | | | **6.22** | **10.00** |

## Hastings Link

| | | | Miles | Km |
|---|---|---|---|---|
| Hastings (T.I.C.) | to | Glebe Wood | 3.9 | 6.3 |
| Glebe Wood | to | Doleham Ditch | 3.5 | 5.6 |
| | | | **7.4** | **11.9** |

# ANIMALS, BIRDS AND FLOWERS

Throughout this walk there is an abundance of wildlife, birds and flowers to be seen. The low lying land between Pevensey and Bexhill formed a shallow harbour in 1066, but now it is marsh land in parts. Apart from sheep and cattle, you can also find badgers, foxes, frogs, rabbits, voles, hedgehogs and field mice.

Out of 160 British species of aquatic flowering plants, 110 of them grow in the area. These include yellow water iris, water dropwort and great reed mace. The predominantly low level and marshy ground provides excellent terrain for water birds and other species. You may see herons, ducks, plovers, redshanks, warblers, swans, greebes, wagtails and sandpipers. Woodland birds include cuckoo, woodpecker, jackdaw, grouse, robin and swallows.

Walking as quietly as possible you can see and hear the rich diversity of plant and animal life in the fields, hedgerows, woodland and on the riverbank. You may even see a fox, as I did near Crowhurst.

## ATTRACTIONS ON ROUTE

Plan your journey to include some of the attractions on or very near the 1066 route.

**Pevensey**
Pevensey Castle                                    01323 762604

**Herstmonceux**
Science Centre & Discovery Park         01323 832731
www.science-project.org
Herstmonceux Castle  (Gardens only)     01323 833816

**Battle**
Museum of Local History                   01424 775955
Buckley's Yesterday's World               01424 775378
The Almonry & Town Model                 01424 772210
Abbey & Battlefield                       01424 773792
Church of St. Mary the Virgin            01424 773649
Golf Course                              01424 775677
Battle re-enactment around 14/15 October -
Contact Battle T.I.C for details.        01424 773721

**Westfield**
Carr Taylor Vineyards                    01424 752501

**Winchelsea**
Court Hall Museum                        01797 224395
Strand Gate
St. Thomas' Church

**Rye**
Heritage Centre, Story of Rye            01797 226696
Castle Museum                            01797 226728
St. Mary's Church                        01797 222430

| Treasury of Mechanical Music | 01797 223345 |
| Art Galleries | 01797 222433/223218 |
| Harbour Nature Reserve & Camber Castle | 01797 223862 |
| The Landgate (Medieval Gateway c. 1329) | |
| Mermaid St. & Inn | |
| Lamb House | |
| Guided Tour of Rye | 01797 226696 |

## Hastings

| Smugglers Adventure | 01424 422964 |
| Underwater World | 01424 718776 |
| Shipwreck Heritage Centre | 01424 437452 |
| Fisherman's Museum | 01424 461446 |
| Old Town Hall Museum | 01424 781166 |
| Museum & Art Gallery | 01424 781155 |
| East Hill Cliff Railway | 01424 781111 |
| West Hill Cliff Railway | 01424 781111 |
| Hastings Castle (West Hill) | 01424 781111 |
| Bus Tour | 01424 781111 |
| Hastings Embroidery | 01424 781010 |
| Hastings Country Park | |

## Bexhill

| Museum of Costume & Social History | 01424 210045 |
| Bexhill Museum | 01424 787950 |
| De La Warr Pavilion | 01424 787900 |
| Leisure Pool | 01424 731508 |
| Old Town | |
| St. Peter's Parish Church | |
| Manor Gardens | |
| Motor Racing Heritage Centre | |

## TOURIST INFORMATION CENTRES (TICs)

Planning a visit to 1066 Country? These offices offer a comprehensive service to visitors.

### Battle
88 High Street ,Battle TN33 9AQ
Tel. 01424 773721  Fax. 01424 773436
Email  battletic@rother.gov.uk
Website  www.battletown.co.uk

### Bexhill
51 Marina, Bexhill-on-Sea TN40 1BQ
Tel. 01424 732208  Fax. 01424 212500
Email  bexhilltic@rother.gov.uk
Website  www.bexhill.org.

### Hastings
Queens Square, Priory Meadow, Hastings TN34 1TL
Tel. 01424 781111  Fax 01424 781186
Email  hic_info@hastings.gov.uk
Website  www.hastings.gov.uk

Fishmarket, The Stade, Old Town, Hastings
Tel. 01424 781111(summer)

### Rye
The Heritage Centre, Strand Quay, Rye TN31 7AY
Tel. 01797 226696
Email  ryetic@rother.gov.uk
Website  www.rye.org.uk

### Boship
Boship Roundabout, Lower Dicker, Hailsham BN23 4DT
Tel/Fax. 01323 442667

### 1066 Country Walk
Website  www.1066country.com

## PUBLIC HOUSES ON ROUTE

(within easy walking distance of the 1066 Country Walk)

- The Smugglers Inn, Pevensey
- The Royal Oak, Pevensey
- The Lamb Inn, Wartling
- The Bulls Head, Boreham Street
- Ash Tree Inn, Brownbread Street
- The White Hart, Catsfield
- The Inn at Crowhurst, Crowhurst
- The Plough, Crowhurst
- The New Inn, Westfield
- The Plough Inn, Westfield
- The Queens Head, Icklesham
- Robin Hood Inn, Icklesham
- The Oast House Inn, Icklesham
- The New Inn, Winchelsea
- The Bridge Inn, Winchelsea
- The Three Oaks, Three Oaks
- White Hart Inn, Guestling

Plus many pubs to choose from in and around Battle, Bexhill, Hastings and Rye, too numerous to include them all by name.

## POST WALK

On completing your historic walk through time on the 1066 Country Walk, you may like a souvenir to mark your achievement. The author has produced a certificate and cloth badge. The certificate is priced at 55p and the cloth badge (similar to the waymark signs) at £3.30. These are available, post free from:

**Brian Smailes,**
**Challenge Publications**
**7, Earlsmere Drive,**
**Ardsley,**
**Barnsley,**
**S. Yorks,**
**S71 5HH**

Visit our website at :-
www.chall-pub.fsnet.co.uk
Email - challengepublications@yahoo.co.uk

The author would be pleased to receive any comments regarding the walk, especially details of any unusual attempts e.g. dressed in 1066 battle dress. Should you or your group be intending this, then please be aware of your safety, the weather conditions and time of year you are doing the walk.

# USEFUL ADDRESSES / TELEPHONE NUMBERS

**Long Distance Walkers Association**
Brian Smith
10 Temple Park Close, Leeds LS15 0JJ
Tel: 0113 2642205

This association is set up to further the interests of those who enjoy long distance walking. Members receive a journal three times each year which includes information on all aspects of long distance walking.

**Ramblers Association**
2nd Floor, Camelford House, 87-90,
Albert Embankment, London SE1 7TW
Local groups with regular meetings.

**East Sussex County Council**
Rights of Way
Tel: 01273 481000

**Rye Bay Countryside Rangers**
Host guided walks and cycle rides
Tel: 01797 226488 for further details

**East Sussex Public Transport Helpline**
Tel: 01273 474747

**Traveline (West Sussex)**
Tel: 0345 959099

**National Rail Enquiries**
Tel: 0345 484950

**National Express**
Tel: 0990 808080

# GLOSSARY OF WORDS

**B &B** - Bed and breakfast.

**Bearing** - A degree or number of degrees set on a compass then follow the direction of travel arrow to walk on that bearing to reach your intended destination.

**Col** - A pass or saddle between two hills. It provides access between one valley and another.

**Dyke, Dike, Ditch** - Words used to denote a long ridge of earth or a water channel either raised up or below normal level.

**Grid Reference** - Derived from the National grid reference system. This is used to pinpoint a place on a map by the use of letters and numbers, written as  G.R. _ _ _ _ _ _

**Kissing Gate** - Swing gate that usually lets one person through at a time by moving the gate backwards and forwards.

**Magnetic Bearing** - This is a grid bearing taken from a map and the relevant magnetic variation added to it to obtain the magnetic bearing. See the relevant maps for details of current magnetic variation.

**Metalled Road** - Generally known as a stone chipping road. This term evolved and became known as the roads metal or the roads surface.

**Path** - A narrow path of grass, mud, stone, etc., suitable for walkers. Not usually more than 2m wide.

**Plateau** - A wide and mainly flat area of elevated land.

**Summit** - The highest point of a mountain or hill.

**T.I.C**. - Tourist information centre.

**Track** - A road (possibly rough) usually wide enough for a vehicle and often leading to a farm.

**Trig Point** - True name is triangulation pillar. These mark the summit of many mountains, but not every mountain has one. It is a small stone pillar with a number on it. The height of the mountain is taken from this point.

**Waymarker** - A term used in this book  to  denote the path direction. This walk is well marked with small 1066 discs on stiles, posts, signposts, fences and kissing gates.
Red discs on main route with white arrow. White discs on Bexhill and Hastings Links with red arrow (see introduction).

# NOTES